S0-BFD-561

Author:

Ian Graham studied applied physics at City University in London. He then received a graduate degree in journalism, specializing in science and technology. Since becoming a freelance author and journalist, he has written more than 100 children's nonfiction books.

Artist:

David Antram was born in Brighton, England, in 1958. He studied at Eastbourne College of Art and then worked in advertising for 15 years before becoming a full-time artist. He has illustrated many children's nonfiction books.

Series creator:

David Salariya was born in Dundee, Scotland. He has illustrated a wide range of books and has created and designed many new series for publishers in the UK and overseas. David established The Salariya Book Company in 1989. He lives in Brighton with his wife, illustrator Shirley Willis, and their son, Jonathan.

Editor: **Stephen Haynes**

Editorial Assistant: **Mark Williams**

PAPER FROM
SUSTAINABLE
FORESTS

© The Salariya Book Company Ltd MMXIII

No part of this publication may be reproduced in whole or in part, or stored in a retrieval system, or transmitted in any form by any means, electronic, mechanical, photocopying, recording or otherwise, without written permission of the publisher. For information regarding permission, write to the copyright holder.

Published in Great Britain in 2013 by
The Salariya Book Company Ltd
25 Marlborough Place, Brighton BN1 1UB

ISBN-13: 978-0-531-25943-6 (lib. bdg.)   978-0-531-23040-4 (pbk.)

All rights reserved.
Published in 2013 in the United States
by Franklin Watts
An imprint of Scholastic Inc.
Published simultaneously in Canada.

A CIP catalog record for this book is available
from the Library of Congress.

Printed and bound in Shanghai, China.
Printed on paper from sustainable sources.
Reprinted in MMXVII.
3 4 5 6 7 8 9 10 R 22 21 20 19 18 17

SCHOLASTIC, FRANKLIN WATTS, and associated logos are trademarks and/or registered trademarks of Scholastic Inc., 557 Broadway, New York, NY 10012.

This book is sold subject to the conditions that it shall not, by way of trade or otherwise, be lent, resold, hired out, or otherwise circulated without the publisher's prior consent in any form or binding or cover other than that in which it is published and without similar condition being imposed on the subsequent purchaser.

You Wouldn't Want to Be Sir Isaac Newton!

Written by
Ian Graham

Illustrated by
David Antram

Created and designed by
David Salariya

A Lonely Life You'd Rather Not Lead

Franklin Watts®
An Imprint of Scholastic Inc.
NEW YORK • TORONTO • LONDON • AUCKLAND • SYDNEY
MEXICO CITY • NEW DELHI • HONG KONG
DANBURY, CONNECTICUT

Contents

Introduction

You are one of the most famous scientists of the seventeenth century—perhaps the greatest scientist of *any* century. The laws of nature you discover cause a revolution in science and technology that will help to create the modern world. You will be thought of as the father of modern science. You set the standards for all the scientists who come after you. You are Sir Isaac Newton.

In addition to being a great scientist, you are a Member of Parliament, and you run the Royal Mint. Behind closed doors, you secretly study alchemy, an ancient practice that has more to do with sorcery than science. You also have unusual religious beliefs that put your career at risk.

YOU ARE a remarkable person, but you have trouble getting along with other people. Your obsessions, quarrels, and secrets make you lonely and unhappy.

Childhood

You are born on Christmas Day, 1642, in the village of Woolsthorpe-by-Colsterworth in Lincolnshire, England. Your family is quite well off. Your grandfather, Robert, bought the family home, Woolsthorpe Manor, in 1623. You are named Isaac after your father, who died before you were born. You are a premature baby. It is feared that you may not survive. You are so small that your mother, Hannah, says you would have fit in a quart* mug. When you are just three years old, your widowed mother remarries and leaves home to be with her new husband. You are left behind. You miss your mother dreadfully.

*An English quart is equal to 2.4 U.S. pints, or about 1.1 liters.

Welcome to the world, Isaac.

Handy Hint
Make lots of friends when you're young. Some of your childhood friendships will last a lifetime.

ABANDONED! When your mother marries Reverend Barnabas Smith, he doesn't want you with them. You spend the next seven years living with your grandmother, Margery.

THE ENGLISH CIVIL WAR began in the year of your birth. You sometimes see troops riding up and down the roads around your home.

WHEN YOUR STEPFATHER DIES your mother returns to Woolsthorpe with her three new children: Hannah, Benjamin, and Mary. They are your half-sisters and half-brother. You inherit your stepfather's books.

School Days

In 1654, you enroll at Grantham Grammar School. You are a good student and you do well, but after a few years your mother takes you out of school to be trained as a farmer. Education is expensive, and farmers don't need qualifications.

Luckily for science, you are a terrible farmer! You are much more interested in making models and reading books than doing your farm work. When you are supposed to be watching over sheep and pigs, you let them stray into neighbors' fields and gardens. Eventually the headmaster persuades your mother to send you back to school.

Hey! That's my corn!

Handy Hint

If you want to be a great scientist, pay attention at school, work hard, and pass your exams.

GRANTHAM is too far away for you to travel to every day, so you stay there with the local apothecary. His mysterious liquids and potions awaken your interest in science.

AT SCHOOL you carve your name into every bench you sit on. You carve it into a stone window ledge, too.

IN 1658, you measure the strength of the wind during a storm. You see how far you can jump when you leap into the wind and how far you can jump in the opposite direction. Then you compare these to the lengths of jumps on a calm day.

SUNDIALS fascinate you. You carve several of them in stone. You also make simple ones by banging a peg into a wall and marking the hours as the peg's shadow moves around.

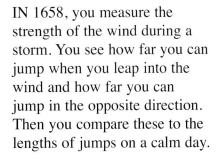

Munch munch

The Plague Years

You do so well at school that you go on to study at Cambridge University. You attend Trinity College as a sizar—a student who pays lower fees, or none at all, in return for work. In 1665, the university closes because of the Great Plague, a deadly disease that sweeps through England. You return to Woolsthorpe Manor, where you do your most important work. While you are thinking about what keeps the moon and planets in their orbits, you see an apple falling from a tree to the ground. This leads to your theory of gravitation.

Soon after you return to Trinity College, you become a professor of mathematics at the age of only 26.

STUDYING LIGHT. You use a wedge of glass called a prism to split white light into a rainbowlike spectrum of colors.

MOST SCIENTISTS think that light is made of waves of energy, but you think it is made of particles. Later, scientists will discover that light consists of bundles of energy, called photons, that display both wavelike and particle-like properties.

Handy Hint

Avoid the plague and other nasty diseases. Stay away from cities where people live crowded together.

Hmmm...

YOU STUDY the orbits of comets. The Great Comet of 1680 is so bright that it can be seen even in daylight.

IN THE LATE 1660s, you make the first successful reflecting telescope. Instead of using lenses to magnify distant objects, a reflecting telescope has a curved mirror. Your 6-inch (15-centimeter) reflecting telescope has the magnifying power of a 6-foot (2-meter) telescope with lenses.

Newton the Alchemist

Seventeenth-century science is intermingled with alchemy—a study steeped in myth and magic. You spend a great deal of time doing secret alchemical research. One of the things alchemists try to do is to find a substance called the philosopher's stone, which is supposed to be able to change cheap metals, such as lead, into precious metals such as gold. But alchemists also invented some of the processes that would be used later by scientists. You use one of these processes, distillation, to separate liquids from each other. You heat a mixture until one of the liquids evaporates, then collect the vapor and cool it to change it back to a liquid. You keep detailed notes of your experiments.

SOME OF the brightly colored pigments used by artists were discovered or invented by alchemists.

Take twice a day with water.

"Saturn's child is the serpent which devours Cadmus."

ALCHEMISTS discovered medications that were based on chemical compounds instead of plants—laying the foundations of modern medicine.

BOOKS ABOUT ALCHEMY are often written in a code that hides their meaning. You spend hours deciphering them so that you can repeat their experiments.

Newton's Books

You write two of the most important science books ever written. The first is *Philosophiae Naturalis Principia Mathematica* (Latin for "mathematical principles of natural philosophy"), or *Principia* for short. The astronomer Edmund Halley urges you to finish writing it and then pays for it to be published. It contains your laws of motion and gravity, and other laws governing the motion of the planets.

The second book, *Opticks*, deals with light and color. In these books you describe your experiments in detail and use mathematics to prove your theories. This process eventually becomes the standard way of doing science.

SEVERAL YEARS' WORTH of notes and calculations go up in smoke when your laboratory at Trinity College catches fire during the winter of 1677 to 1678.

Worth every penny!

Handy Hint

Take good care of your work. If you lose it, it could take you years to replace it.

MOST OF THE WORK described in your book *Opticks* was done by the 1670s, but you delay publishing it until 1704, when your main critic and rival, the scientist Robert Hooke, is dead.

Bill

OPTICKS:
OR, A
TREATISE
OF THE
REFLEXIONS, REFRACTIONS,
INFLEXIONS and COLOURS
OF
LIGHT.
ALSO
TWO TREATISES
OF THE
SPECIES and MAGNITUDE
OF
Curvilinear Figures

MDCCIV

Edmund Halley

Making a Mint

By the end of the seventeenth century, the coins used in England are worn and misshapen. Some of them are more than 100 years old, and many of them are counterfeit. The government decides to take all the coins out of circulation and replace them with new ones.

You have been looking for something new to do, so you are very pleased to be put in charge of the project. You are appointed warden of the Royal Mint, and later its master. You pursue counterfeiters and make sure that they are taken to court. Counterfeiting coins is a capital crime—those who are caught can be executed.

Gulp!

SOME COINS are made of valuable metals such as gold and silver. People sometimes steal the metal by clipping pieces off their edges.

THE NEW COINS produced by the mint have milled (ridged) edges. It is easy to see if these coins have been clipped. If they have, they are no longer accepted as payment.

Handy Hint

When coins are in short supply, try bartering (swapping goods).

Get on with it—hang the counterfeiter!

"You're a dead man, Newton!"

Cost of alloy per lb for making coins:

12d

YOU ARE FEARED and hated by the coin clippers and counterfeiters. You receive death threats, but that doesn't stop you from pursuing them.

YOU KNOW all about melting metal from your alchemical work. So you know exactly how much it costs to produce the metal needed for making new coins. You force the metal suppliers to lower their prices.

Arise, Sir Isaac

Being the greatest scientist who ever lived *and* master of the Royal Mint doesn't occupy all of your life. You find the time to be a politician, too. You are invited to be the Member of Parliament for Cambridge University in 1689. You send detailed reports back to the university from Parliament, but you never make any speeches yourself. When you are elected to a second term in 1701, you resign from your professorship at Cambridge. In 1703, you become president of the Royal Society. Two years later you are knighted and so become *Sir* Isaac Newton, the first scientist ever to receive this honor.

Shut that window, please.

WHEN YOU FEEL a cold draft in the House of Commons one day, you ask a nearby usher to close a window. This is the only thing history records you saying during all of your time in Parliament.

YOU ARE KNIGHTED by Queen Anne during a royal visit to your old college at Cambridge University.

Handy Hint

You'll find out who your friends are when you run for election to Parliament.

VOTE FOR ME

Mr. President!

THE ROYAL SOCIETY was formed in 1660 by a group of leading scientists so that they could meet to discuss their work.

IT'S FASHIONABLE for important people like you to be seen at the opera. However, you go to see an opera only once. You are so bored by it that you never go again.

Picking Fights

You are a difficult man to get along with. You have arguments with several of the most important mathematicians and scientists of your time. You hate anyone criticizing your work. You also fail to give other people credit when you make use of their work. Your archrival is Robert Hooke, one of the most brilliant scientists of the age.

YOU NEVER RUN AWAY from a fight. When you were a boy, a bully attacked you at school, and you fought back and won. Not satisfied with beating the bully in a fight, you worked harder until you beat him at schoolwork, too.

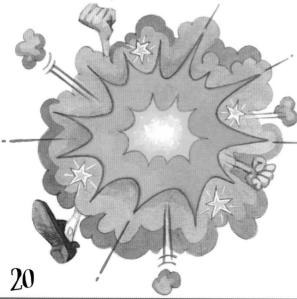

GOTTFRIED LEIBNIZ is a brilliant mathematician, famous for inventing a mathematical method called calculus. He is unaware that you have already developed your own version of calculus. The two of you argue over who was first.

This is an outrage, sir!

You, sir, are a scoundrel!

Handy Hint

Make sure you get the credit for your great ideas by publishing the results before anyone else does.

ROBERT HOOKE criticizes your work on light and claims some of the credit for your theory of gravity. You never forgive him. Hooke's portrait mysteriously disappears from the Royal Society while you are the society's president. Many of Hooke's notes and equipment vanish at the same time.

JOHN FLAMSTEED, the Astronomer Royal, produces a huge catalog of stars that he plans to publish one day. He is furious when you, tired of waiting for him to do it, go ahead and publish a copy of the catalog that is full of errors.

21

Heresy

WHEN YOU ARE AWARDED your bachelor of arts and master of arts degrees, you have to sign a document to say that you accept the teachings of the Anglican Church. But later, your beliefs change.

Xou are a deeply religious man, but you have unusual beliefs that cause problems. You study religion with the same obsessive attention to detail that you apply to your scientific work. You read the Bible and other ancient writings on religion and make extensive notes. In fact, you write more about religion than science.

YOU APPEAL to King Charles II for permission to become a professor without having to take holy orders. You have little hope of success, but surprisingly the king agrees. Your career can continue.

THE END IS NIGH

It's not that nigh.

HOLY BIBLE

YOU USE events described in the Bible to figure out when the world will end. You calculate that the end of the world will not happen until after 2060.

In seventeenth-century England, important academic figures like you are expected to take holy orders and become ministers of religion. As a result of your research, you no longer accept all the teachings of the church, making it impossible for you to take holy orders. This could end your career!

Handy Hint

Friends in high places can be very useful when you need some help.

Under Pressure

Y ou often suffer from depression. You also find it stressful to keep your alchemical research and your religious beliefs secret. You crack under the pressure and suffer two nervous breakdowns. The first happens in 1678, probably as a result of constant arguments with other scientists. Your second breakdown, in 1693, is much more serious. The first sign of trouble is noticed by your friend Samuel Pepys* (famous today for his diary). He is so worried by a rambling letter from you that he asks friends to visit you to make sure you are all right. This breakdown ends your scientific research, and you work as a government official for the rest of your life.

pronounced "Peeps"

What Made You Sick?

NO ONE REALLY KNOWS, but there are several possibilities. You blame insomnia (inability to sleep). Sometimes you go several days without sleeping.

IN 1693, you argue with the Swiss mathematician Nicolas Fatio de Duillier (right), ending your friendship. He was one of the very few close friends you ever had.

YOUR HEALTH may have been damaged by years of breathing in poisonous fumes from the alchemical compounds you experimented with, especially mercury.

Whatever is the matter with him?

Samuel Pepys

Handy Hint

Try to get plenty of sleep at night, or you won't be able to concentrate during the day.

YOU WORRY that if your unusual religious beliefs were to become known by everyone, fellow scientists and all of society would shun you.

YOU FEEL FRUSTRATED at times when you can't make any progress with your work.

YOU ARE A HYPOCHONDRIAC. You constantly worry about your health and fear you are suffering from one illness or another. You take medicines that probably do more harm than good.

25

Old Age

Your health begins to fail in the early 1720s. You suffer from a violent cough, inflammation of the lungs, painful bouts of gout, and kidney stones. A trip to London on March 2, 1727, exhausts you and you become bedridden. You drift in and out of a coma for the next two weeks. Friends and colleagues come to visit you for the last time. When a priest arrives to give you the last rites, you send him away. Your life ends on March 20. You leave almost £32,000, which is divided among your eight nephews and nieces.

IN 1697, your 17-year-old niece, Catherine Barton, came to London to work as your housekeeper. She continues to take care of you into your old age.

I don't need a priest.

Leave your descendants a grisly present by having a death mask molded from your face just after you die.

YOUR BODY is buried under the floor of Westminster Abbey in London. In 1731, a monument is placed near your grave (left). Many years later, other famous scientists, including Charles Darwin, are buried here, too. This part of the church becomes known as Scientists' Corner.

HIC DEPOSITUM EST
QUOD MORTALE FUIT
ISAACI NEWTONI*

Here lies that which was mortal of Isaac Newton.

27

Newton's Legacy

YOU IMAGINE a huge cannon being fired from the top of a tall mountain. Gravity will make the cannonball fall to the ground (1).

But if the cannon were powerful enough, the cannonball would "fall" all the way around the world (2). In this thought experiment you have foreseen a spacecraft orbiting the Earth!

You will be remembered as one of the greatest of all scientists. Your work enables those who come after you to achieve even greater things, just as you built upon the work of the great thinkers who lived before you. You changed physics from debates between philosophers into a real science based on experiments, observations, and theories with mathematical proofs. However, you had few friends and you never married, so your great achievements came at great personal cost.

*If I have seen further, it is by standing on the shoulders of giants.**

* Newton recognized that the work of earlier thinkers had made it possible for him to develop his own more advanced theories.

THE LAWS and principles that you figured out and the scientific methods you used made the Industrial Revolution possible.

DESCARTES

HALLEY

G. Leibniz

HUYGENS

J. Flamsteed

R. Hooke

We should call the unit of force the newton.

WHEN SCIENTISTS in the twentieth century are looking for a new name for a metric unit of force, they choose to name it the newton. One newton is the force that makes a 1-kilogram mass accelerate at 1 meter per second per second.

ROCKETS are an example of your third law of motion: "To every action there is an equal and opposite reaction." This means that the rocket pushes burning fuel out in one direction and the fuel pushes back, thrusting the rocket in the opposite direction.

YOUR ACHIEVEMENTS are recognized by the Bank of England in 1978 when it issues a one-pound note with your face on it.

Glossary

Alchemy An early form of science that combined useful experiments, ancient myths, and mistaken beliefs.

Anglican Church The national Christian church of England.

Apothecary An old name for a pharmacist, a person who makes and sells medicines.

Astronomer Royal The leading astronomer in England (and, later, the United Kingdom), who advised the king or queen on scientific matters.

Calculus A branch of mathematics concerned with the study of changing quantities such as the position, speed, and acceleration of moving objects.

Clipping Cutting a small piece of precious metal off a coin in order to steal the metal for profit.

Coma A state of unconsciousness from which a person cannot be woken.

Comet A mountain of rock, dust, and ice flying through space around the sun. If comets fly close to the sun, some of their ice vaporizes, releasing gas and dust, which form long tails.

Counterfeiter A criminal who makes illegal copies of something, such as coins or banknotes.

Death mask A face molded in wax or plaster from the actual face of a person immediately after he or she has died.

Distillation A method of separating or purifying liquids by heating them until they evaporate. The vapor is then cooled to change it back into a liquid.

English Civil War A war between the supporters of King Charles I (Royalists or Cavaliers) and the supporters of the English Parliament (Parliamentarians or Roundheads). It lasted from 1642 to 1651 and ended in victory for the Parliamentarians, who executed the king.

Grammar school A school that offered a more academic education than other types of school. The best students went on to the church or a university.

Heresy A religious belief that disagrees with the teachings of a church.

Holy orders The rite of being made a Christian minister. Someone who has become a priest or minister is said to have taken holy orders.

House of Commons The lower house of the English (later British) Parliament.

Hypochondriac A person who is constantly worried about his or her health.

Industrial Revolution The period between about 1750 and 1850, when new inventions such as the steam engine, factories, and railroads changed Britain and then other countries from farming nations to industrial nations.

Last rites Prayers said for, and in the presence of, someone who is dying, to prepare him or her for the afterlife.

Member of Parliament A person elected by voters to represent them in their country's lawmaking assembly.

Milled (coins) Produced by a machine that gives coins a ridged edge, so it is easy to see if they have been clipped.

Natural philosophy The study of nature and the universe, before the modern science of physics began.

Plague A deadly infectious disease carried by rats and spread to humans by fleas.

Premature baby A baby that is born before it is fully developed. In earlier centuries, premature babies rarely survived.

Royal Mint The organization in Britain that produces (mints) coins.

Royal Society A club or association, formed in 1660, where leading scientists meet, exchange ideas, and encourage the use of science for the benefit of humanity.

Sundial A device that shows the time by using the changing position of the sun in the sky to cast a shadow on a scale marked with the hours of the day.

Index